Glamour Knits

15 sensuous designs to knit and keep forever

ERIKA KNIGHT
COLLECTIBLES

photography by Katya de Grunwald

POTTER
CRAFT

New York

Editorial director Jane O'Shea
Creative director Helen Lewis
Designer Claire Peters
Project editor Lisa Pendreigh
Editorial assistant Andrew Bayliss
Pattern checkers Eva Yates and Sally Harding
Photographer Katya de Grunwald
Photographer's assistant Amy Gwatkin
Stylist Beth Dadswell
Hair and make-up artist Anita Keeling
Model Laure Brosson at Select Model Management
Production director Vincent Smith
Production controller Ruth Deary

Published in the United States by
Potter Craft, an imprint of the Crown
Publishing Group, a division of Random
House, Inc., New York.

www.crownpublishing.com
www.pottercraft.com

POTTER CRAFT and
CLARKSON N. POTTER
are trademarks and
POTTER and colophon are registered
trademarks of Random House, Inc.

Originally published in Great Britain by
Quadrille Publishing Limited, London.

The rights of Erika Knight to be identified as
the author of this work have been asserted by
her in accordance with the Copyright,
Designs, and Patents Act 1988.

Library of Congress Cataloging-in-Publication
Data is available.

ISBN-13: 978-0-307-34720-6
ISBN-10: 0-307-34720-6

Printed and bound in China

10 9 8 7 6 5 4 3 2 1

First Potter Craft Edition

introduction

Glamour is a must-have portfolio of sensuous knits inspired by Hollywood sirens. Knitwear has never looked so sexy; these garments all provide an easy glamour for both day and evening wear by combining slinky shapes with sumptuous textures. Knit a chevron sweater in mercerized cotton to team with either a clingy pencil skirt or favorite jeans, or indulge yourself in a lacy knit shrug tied with a shiny ribbon to slip over a delicate camisole. Yarns are sensuous, tactile, and opulent: velvet chenille, flowing satin, and sensuous silk. The collection is worked in a seductive palette of palest pink, ripe peach, and delicate pastel green through to rich teal, gold, plum, and grape, and beautifully trimmed with lace and ribbon, or embroidered and beaded embellishments.

the
glamour
collection

the patterns

sequined scarf

materials

Any super-fine-weight metallic yarn or super-fine-weight
  mercerized cotton yarn, such as Rowan *Lurex Shimmer* or
  Yeoman's *Cotton Cannele 4ply*
  Two ¾ oz (25g) balls
Pair of size 3 (3.25mm) knitting needles
Lace, sequins, and satin ribbon for trimmings, each approximately
  1¾–2 yds (1.6–1.8m) long

size

One size, approximately 55 in (140cm) long by 3¼ in (8cm) wide

gauge

29 sts and 41 rows = 4 in (10cm) in St st using size 3 (3.25mm) needles
  or whatever size necessary to obtain gauge

See pages 10–11

sequined scarf

pattern notes

- Both ends of the scarf have the same broken "ladders."
- The dropped sts form the ladders. Make sure they drop to the bottom of the ladder, which is the "make 1" st. The center ladder runs the length of the scarf, and the others are random.
- The ladders tend to close up after the stitch is dropped, so pull them apart if they seem to have disappeared.

To make scarf

Using size 3 (3.25mm) needles, cast on 2 sts.

Row 1 (RS): K to last st, k into front and back of last st.

Row 2: K into front and back of first st, p to last st, k1—*4 sts.*

Rep last 2 rows twice more—*8 sts.*

Next row (RS): K4, M1, k to last st, k into front and back of last st—*10 sts.*

Work in St st **and at the same time** k first and last st of all rows throughout, and cont as foll:

Work 3 rows, inc 1 st on every row as set (1 st at end of every k row and at beg of every p row)—*13 sts.*

Next row (RS): K9, M1, k to last st, k into front and back of last st—*15 sts.*

Work 3 rows, inc 1 st on every row as set—*18 sts.*

Next row (RS): K14, M1, k to end—*19 sts.*

Note: Shaping at this end of scarf is now complete and M1 sts that start ladders have been made.

Work even for 19 rows.

Next row (RS): K4, drop next st, k9, drop next st, k to end—*17 sts.*

Work even for 9 rows.

Next row (RS): K4, M1, k9, M1, k to end—*19 sts.*

Work even for 23 rows.

Next row (RS): K4, drop next st, k9, drop next st, k to end—*17 sts.*

Work even for 9 rows.

Next row (RS): K4, M1, k9, M1, k to end—*19 sts.*

Work even for 23 rows.

Next row (RS): K4, drop next st, k9, drop next st, k to end—*17 sts.*

Cont on these 17 sts until scarf measures approximately 44½ in (113cm) from cast-on edge, ending with RS facing for next row.

Next row (RS): K4, M1, k9, M1, k to end—*19 sts.*

Work even for 23 rows.

Next row (RS): K4, drop next st, k9, drop next st, k to end—*17 sts.*

Work even for 9 rows.

Next row (RS): K4, M1, k9, M1, k to end—*19 sts.*

Work even for 23 rows.
Next row (RS): K4, drop next st, k9, drop next st, k to end—*17 sts.*
Work even for 9 rows.
Next row (RS): K4, M1, k9, M1, k to end—*19 sts.*
Work even for 19 rows.
Shape end
Next row (RS): K2tog, k2, drop next st, k to end—*17 sts.*
Work 3 rows, dec 1 st at end of every p row and at beg of every k row by working k2tog—*14 sts.*
Next row (RS): K2tog, k2, drop next st, work to end—*12 sts.*
Work 3 rows, dec 1 st on every row as set (1 st at end of every p row and at beg of every k row)—*9 sts.*

Next row (RS): K2tog, k2, drop next st, k to end—*7 sts.*
Cont dec as set until 2 sts rem.
Next row: K2tog.
Fasten off.

To finish
Thread a length of trimming through long ladders, fasten securely, and allow extra length to create a fringe. Thread shorter ladders in same way. Alternatively, leave ladders and trim wide spaces between ladder sts.

ribbed shrug

materials

Any medium-weight wool yarn, such as Rowan *Soft Baby*
7 (7, 8) × 1¾ oz (50g) balls
Pair each of sizes 10½ (7mm) and 11 (8mm) knitting needles
Size 10½ (7mm) circular knitting needle

sizes

to fit bust	32–34	36–38	40–42	in
	81–86	91–97	102–107	cm
actual length	17¾	18½	19¼	in
	45	47	49	cm
cuff to cuff	59¾	61¾	63¾	in
	152	157	162	cm

gauge

12 sts and 16 rows = 4 in (10cm) in St st using size 11 (8mm) needles or whatever size necessary to obtain gauge and two strands of yarn held together

To make shrug (made in one piece)
Using size 10½ (7mm) needles and two strands of yarn tog, cast on 32 (36: 40) sts.
Rib row 1: *K1, p1, rep from * to end.
Rep last row until shrug measures 6 in (15cm) from cast-on edge.
First size only
Next row: *K1, p into front and back of next st, rep from * to end.
Second and third sizes only
Next row: K1, p1, *k1, p into front and back of next st, rep from * to last 2 sts, k1, p1—*48 (52: 58) sts.*
Change to size 11 (8mm) needles and work in rib patt as foll:
Row 1 (RS): *K3, p2, rep from * to last 3 sts, k3.
Row 2: *P3, k2, rep from * to last 3 sts, p3.
Rep these 2 rows until shrug measures 55¾ (55¾: 57¾)in (137: 142: 147)cm from cast-on edge, ending with RS facing for next row.
Change to 10½ (7mm) needles.
First size only
Next row (RS): *K1, k2tog, rep from * to end.
Second and third sizes only
Next row (RS): K2, *k1, k2tog, rep from * to last 2 sts, k2—*32 (36: 38) sts.*
Work 6 in (15cm) in k1, p1 rib.
Bind off in rib.

To finish
Place markers at both sides of work 21 in (53cm) in from each cuff.
Fold work in half lengthwise and sew cuff and sleeve seam to markers, leaving center 17¾ (19¾: 21¾)in (46: 51: 56)cm unsewn.
Using 10½ (7mm) circular needle and two strands of yarn tog and with RS facing, pick up and k 150 (162: 180) sts evenly around opening.
Working in rounds, work 4½ in (12cm) in k1, p1 rib.
Bind off in rib.
Weave in any loose yarn ends.

See pages 12–13

lace top

materials

Any fine-weight mohair yarn, such as Rowan *Kidsilk Haze*
   3 (3, 4, 4, 5, 5) × ¾ oz (25g) balls
Pair each of sizes 2 (3mm) and 3 (3.25mm) knitting needles
Size 3 (3.25mm) circular knitting needle
Six small buttons, approximately ½ in (12mm) in diameter
Scrap of organza fabric, approximately 8 in (20cm) by 1½ in (4cm)
2 yds (1.8m) of matching satin ribbon, 1 in (2.5cm) wide, for tie

sizes

to fit bust	32	34	36	38	40	42	in
	81	86	91	97	102	107	cm
actual bust	32	34	36	38	40	42	in
	81	86	91	97	102	107	cm
length	20	21	21	22	22	23	in
	51	53	53	56	56	59	cm
sleeve seam	2¼	2¾	2¾	2½	3½	3½	in
	6	7	7	7	9	9	cm

gauge

25 sts and 32 rows = 4 in (10cm) in lace patt using size 3 (3.25mm) needles or
   whatever size necessary to obtain gauge

See pages 14–15

lace top

stitches

lace pattern

Row 1 and all odd-numbered rows (WS): P.

Rows 2, 4, and 6 (RS): K1, *yo, skp, k1, k2tog, yo, k1, rep from * to end.

Row 8: K2, *yo, sk2p, yo, k3, rep from * ending last rep with k2 instead of k3.

Row 10: K1, * k2tog, yo, k1, yo, skp, k1, rep from * to end.

Row 12: K2tog, * yo, k3, yo, sk2p, rep from * to last 5 sts, yo, k3, yo, skp.

Rep rows 1–12 to form patt.

Back

Using size 2 (3mm) needles, cast on 103 (109: 115: 121: 127: 133) sts. K 1 row.

Work first 3 rows of lace patt. Change to size 3 (3.25mm) needles and cont in lace patt until back measures 13 (13½: 13½: 14: 14: 14½)in (33: 34: 34: 36: 36: 37)cm from cast-on edge, ending with RS facing for next row.

Shape armholes

Keeping to patt as set throughout, bind off 5 sts at beg of next 2 rows. Dec 1 st each end of next 5 rows, then on foll 6 alt rows—*71 (77: 83: 89: 95: 101) sts.***

Work even until armhole measures 4¾ (5¼: 5¼: 5¾: 5¾: 6)in (12: 13: 13: 14: 14: 15.5)cm, ending with RS facing for next row.

Divide back

Next row (RS): Work 35 (38: 41: 44: 47: 50) sts, then turn, leaving rem sts on a holder.

Work each side separately.

Work even until armhole measures 7 (7½: 7½: 8: 8: 8½)in (18: 19: 19: 20: 20: 22)cm, ending with RS facing for next row.

Shape shoulders and neck

Bind off 6 (7: 8: 8: 9: 10) sts at beg of next row, 12 (13: 14: 14: 14: 15) sts at beg of next row, 6 (7: 8: 9: 10: 10) sts at beg of next row, and 4 (4: 4: 4: 4: 4) sts at beg of next row. Bind off rem 7 (7: 7: 9: 10: 11) sts. With RS facing, rejoin yarn and k2tog, then patt to end—*35 (38: 41: 44: 47: 50) sts.*

Compete to match first side, reversing all shaping.

Front

Work as for back to **.

Work even until armhole measures 4½ (5: 5: 5½: 5½: 5¾)in (11.5: 12.5: 12.5: 13.5: 13.5: 14.5)cm, ending with RS facing for next row.

Shape neck

Next row (RS): Work 25 (27: 29: 32: 35: 37) sts, then turn, leaving rem sts on a holder.

Work each side separately.

Dec 1 st at neck edge on next 2 rows, then on foll 2 alt rows, then on every 4th row until 21 (23: 25: 25: 25: 27) sts rem.

Work even until armhole matches back to shoulder, ending with RS facing for next row.

Shape shoulder

Bind off 6 (7: 8: 8: 9: 10) sts at beg of next row and 6 (7: 8: 9: 10:

10) sts on foll alt row.

Bind off rem 7 (7: 7: 9: 10: 11) sts.

With RS facing, rejoin yarn and bind off center 21 (23: 25: 25: 25: 27) sts, then work to end—25 (27: 29: 32: 35: 37) sts.

Complete to match first side, reversing all shaping.

Sleeves (make 2)

Using size 2 (3mm) needles, cast on 72 (77: 77: 77: 82: 87) sts.

Row 1 (RS): P2, * k3, p2, rep from * to end.

Row 2: K2, * p3, k2, rep from * to end.

Rows 3–4: Rep rows 1–2.

Change to size 3 (3.25mm) needles. Cont in rib patt as set throughout, inc 1 st each end of next row and every foll 4th row until there are 80 (83: 83: 85: 90: 95) sts, taking increased sts into rib.

Work even until sleeve measures 2¼ (2¾: 2¾: 2¾: 3½: 3½)in (6: 7: 7: 7: 9: 9)cm from cast-on edge, ending with RS facing for next row.

Shape cap

Bind off 4 sts at beg next 2 rows— 72 (75: 75: 77: 82: 87) sts.

Dec 1 st each end of next 5 rows— 62 (65: 65: 67: 72: 77) sts.

Dec 1 st each end of foll 3 alt rows, then every foll 4th row until

44 (47: 47: 49: 52: 55) sts rem.

Work even for 1 row.

Dec 1 st each end of next and foll 2 alt rows, then foll 3 rows—32 (35: 35: 37: 40: 43) sts.

Bind off 4 sts at beg of next 2 rows.

Bind off rem 24 (27: 27: 29: 32: 35) sts.

Ruffle

Using size 2 (3mm) needles, cast on 13 sts.

Row 1 (WS): K.

Row 2: P5, turn, k5, turn, p5, k3, p5.

Row 3: K5, turn, p5, turn, p5, k3, p5.

Row 4: K5, turn, p5, turn, k13.

Row 5: P5, turn, k5, turn, k13.

Rep rows 2–5 until ruffle measures 7 in (18cm) from cast-on edge, ending with a WS row.

Bind off.

To finish

Weave in any loose yarn ends.

Press pieces gently using a warm iron over a damp cloth.

Sew both shoulder seams.

Picot edgings

Using size 2 (3mm) circular needle and with RS facing, pick up and k 16 (17: 18: 18: 18: 19) sts along left back neck, 24 sts down left front neck, 21 (23: 25: 25: 25: 27) sts across center front neck, 24 sts up right front neck, 16 (17: 18: 18: 18: 19) sts along right back neck, 24 sts down right side of back slit, and 24 sts up left side of back slit— 149 (153: 157: 157: 157: 161) sts.

Do not turn but work picot edging around neck edge as foll:

Round 1 (RS): Bind off next 3 sts, *sl st on right-hand needle back onto left-hand needle and use to cast on 2 sts using knit cast-on, bind off 5 sts, rep from * to end. Fasten off.

Sew in sleeves.

Sew side and sleeve seams.

Using 3mm circular needle and with RS facing, pick up and k 206 (218: 230: 242: 254: 266) sts around lower edge of garment, then work picot edging as for neck edge.

Sew one button to center back neck edge to fasten through lace patt.

Sew ruffle to center front, gathering it slightly as it is sewn on.

Cut a strip of organza 1½ in (4cm) wide by 6½ in (16.5cm) long, and sew it to top of knitted ruffle, gathering it slightly as it is sewn on as before.

Sew on 5 buttons at regular intervals down length of ruffle.

lace shrug

materials

Any fine-weight 4ply mercerized cotton yarn, such as Yeoman's *Cotton Cannele 4ply*
   One 8¾ oz (250g) cone—or 546 (710, 710) yds (500, 650, 650)m
Pair of size 3 (3.25mm) knitting needles
Approximately 2¼ yds (2m) of satin ribbon, 1½ in (4cm) wide

sizes

to fit bust			
	32–34	36–38	40–42	in
	81–86	91–97	102–107	cm
actual length	15¾	17¼	18	in
	40	44	46	cm
width	22½	26	29	in
	57	66	74	cm

gauge

25 sts and 44 rows = 4 in (10cm) in lace patt using size 3 (3.25mm) needles or whatever size necessary to obtain gauge

To make shrug
Shrug is worked in one piece.
Using size 3 (3.25mm) needles, cast on 145 (163: 181) sts loosely.
Work in lace patt as foll:
Row 1 and all odd-numbered rows (WS): P.
Rows 2, 4, and 6: K1, *yo, skp, k1, k2tog, yo, k1, rep from * to end.
Row 8: K2, *yo, sk2p, k3, rep from * ending last rep with k2 instead of k3.
Row 10: K1, *k2tog, yo, k1, yo, skp, k1, rep from * to end.
Row 12: K2tog, *yo, k3, yo, sk2p, rep from * to last 5 sts, yo, k3, yo, skp.

Rep rows 1–12 until shrug measures 15 (16½: 17¼)in (38: 42: 44)cm from cast-on edge.
Bind off loosely.

To finish
Weave in any loose yarn ends.
Lay work out flat and gently steam.
Picot edgings
Using size 3 (3.25mm) needles and with RS facing, pick up and k 145 (163: 181) sts along cast-on edge of shrug. Work edging as foll:
Picot row: Bind off 3 sts, *slip st on right-hand needle back onto left-

hand needle and use to cast on 2 sts using knit cast-on, bind off 5 sts, rep from * to end. Fasten off.
Work picot edging along bound-off edge in same way.
Work picot edging along each side edge of shrug in same way, but pick up 95 (105: 111) sts.
Sew corner seams on edging.
Cut ribbon into four equal pieces, and sew two pieces each to cast-on edge and bound-off edge 3 in (7.5cm) from side edges.

See pages 16–17

chevron sweater

materials

Any super-fine-weight mercerized cotton yarn, such as Yeoman's
 Cotton Cannele 4ply
 A: One 8¾ oz (250g) cone in beige—or 744 (744, 744, 930, 930, 930) yds (680, 680, 680, 850, 850, 850)m
 B: One 8¾ oz (250g) cone in grey-brown—or 186 (372, 372, 372, 558, 558) yds (170, 340, 340, 340, 510, 510)m
 C: One 8¾ oz (250g) cone in blue—or 372 (558, 558, 558, 558, 558) yds (340, 510, 510, 510, 510, 510)m
 D: One 8¾ oz (250g) cone in pink—or 558 (558, 744, 744, 744, 744) yds (510, 510, 680, 680, 680, 680)m
Any super-fine-weight metallic yarn, such as Rowan *Lurex Shimmer*
 E: One ¾ oz (25g) ball in bronze
 F: One ¾ oz (25g) ball in red
Pair of size 3 (3.25mm) knitting needles
Approximately 1¾ yds (1.5m) of ribbon, 1½ in (3.5cm) wide (optional)

sizes

to fit bust	32	34	36	38	40	42	in
	81	86	91	97	102	107	cm
actual bust	33	36	39	42	46	49	in
	84	92	100	108	116	124	cm
length	23½	24	24½	25½	26½	27	in
	60	61	63	65	67	68.5	cm
sleeve length	17¾	18½	19	19½	19½	20	in
(from center back)	45	47	48	49.5	49.5	51	cm

See pages 18–19

chevron sweater

gauge

41 sts (3 repeats plus 2 sts) = 5 in (13cm) in chevron patt using
   size 3 (3.25mm) needles or whatever size necessary to obtain gauge

stitches

chevron pattern
(worked over multiples of 13 sts plus 2 sts)
Row 1 (RS): *K2, M1, k4, sl 1 knitwise, k2tog, psso, k4, M1,
   rep from * to last 2 sts, k2.
Row 2: P.
Rep these 2 rows to form patt, using colors as instructed on next page.

Back

Using size 3 (3.25mm) needles
and A, cast on 132 (145: 158: 171:
184: 197) sts.
**Work in chevron patt until back
measures 6 in (15cm) from cast-on
edge, ending with RS facing for
next row.
Cont in chevron patt throughout,
working stripes as foll:
Change to E and work 1 row.
Change to B and work 1½ in (4cm),
ending with RS facing for next row.
Change to C and work 3½ in
(9cm), ending with RS facing for
next row.
Change to F and work 1 row.**
Change to D and work until back
measures 13 (13½: 14: 14½: 15:

15½)in (33: 34.5: 35.5: 37: 38: 39)cm
from cast-on edge.
Bind off.

Front

Work exactly as for back.

Sleeves (make 2)

Using size 3 (3.25mm) needles
and A, cast on 171 (171: 184: 184:
197: 197) sts.
Work as for back from ** to **.
Change to D and work until sleeve
measures 17¾ (18½: 19: 19½: 19½:
20)in (45: 47: 48: 49.5: 49.5: 51)cm
from cast-on edge.
Bind off firmly.

To finish

Weave in any loose yarn ends.
Lay pieces out flat and gently steam.
Pin front and back pieces together
and sew side seams.
Fold each sleeve in half and pin
side edge of sleeve to bound-off
edge of body as a yoke, so sleeves
meet at center front and center
back to create V-necklines.
Sew yoke and sleeve seams. Then
sew center front and back V-seams
for about 3 in (7.5cm) from body to
create neck plunge desired.
Cut ribbon in half and sew one
piece to each side of back yoke to
tie into a bow in center back or
front as desired.

long gloves

materials

Any fine-weight mohair yarn, such as Rowan *Kidsilk Haze*
  Two ¾ oz (25g) balls
Pair each of sizes 2 (2.75mm) and 3 (3mm) knitting needles

size

One size, to fit woman's medium hand size

gauge

32 sts and 40 rows = 4 in (10cm) in St st using size 2 (2.75mm) needles
  or whatever size necessary to obtain gauge

See pages 20–21

long gloves

pattern notes
• Use mattress stitch to sew glove finger seams for a neat finish.

Right glove
Using size 3 (3mm) needles, cast on 62 sts very loosely.
Beg with a k row, work in St st, dec 1 st at each end of 3rd row and every foll 8th row until 54 sts rem. Change to size 2 (2.75mm) needles and work even until piece measures 8 in (20cm) from cast-on edge, ending with RS facing for next row.**
Shape thumb
Row 1 (RS): K28, k into front and back of next st, k2, k into front and back of next st, k22—*56 sts.*
Cont in St st throughout, work 3 rows.
Row 5 (RS): K28, k into front and back of next st, k4, k into front and back of next st, k22—*58 sts.*
Work 3 rows.
Cont to inc in same way, inc 2 sts on next row and every foll 4th row until there are 68 sts.
Work 3 rows.

Next row (RS): K46, turn, cast on 2 sts.
Next row: P20, turn, cast on 2 sts.
***Work 2 in (5cm) on these 22 sts, ending with RS facing for next row.
Next row (RS): *K2tog, k2, rep from * to last 2 sts, k2.
Work 1 row.
Next row (RS): *K2tog, rep from * to last st, k1—*9 sts.*
Break off yarn and thread end through these 9 sts. Pull up tightly, secure firmly, and sew thumb seam.
With RS facing, rejoin yarn and pick up and k 6 sts from base of thumb, then k to end—*56 sts.*
Work even until piece measures 1½ in (4cm) from pick-up row, ending with RS facing for next row.
Shape first finger
Next row (RS): K36, turn, cast on 1 st.
Next row: P17, turn, cast on 1 st—*18 sts.*
Work 2½ in (6cm) on these 18 sts,

ending with RS facing for next row.
Next row (RS): *K2tog, k2, * rep from * to last two sts, k2.
Work 1 row.
Next row (RS): *K2tog, rep from * to end—*7 sts.*
Break off yarn and thread end through these 7 sts. Pull up tightly, secure firmly, and sew finger seam.
Shape second finger
With RS facing, rejoin yarn and pick up and k 2 sts from base of first finger, then k7, turn, cast on 1 st.
Next row (WS): P17, turn, cast on 1 st—*18 sts.*
Work 2¾ in (7cm) on these 18 sts, ending with RS facing for next row.
Next row (RS): [K2tog, k2] 4 times, k2.
Work 1 row.
Next row (RS): [K2tog] 7 times—*7 sts.*
Break off yarn and thread end through these 7 sts. Pull up tightly, secure firmly, and sew finger seam.

Shape third finger

With RS facing, rejoin yarn and pick up and k 2 sts from base of second finger, then k7, turn, cast on 1 st.

Next row (WS): P17, turn, cast on 1 st—*18 sts*.

Work 2½ in (6cm) on these 18 sts, ending with RS facing for next row.

Next row (RS): [K2tog, k2] 4 times, k2.

Work 1 row.

Next row (RS): [K2tog] 7 times—*7 sts*.

Break off yarn and thread end through these 7 sts. Pull up tightly, secure firmly, and sew finger seam.

Shape fourth finger

With RS facing, rejoin yarn and pick up and k 4 sts from base of third finger, then k to end.

Next row (WS): P16.

Work 2 in (5cm) on these 16 sts, ending with RS facing for next row.

Next row (RS): [K2tog, k2] 4 times

—*12 sts*.

Work 1 row.

Next row (RS): [K2tog] 6 times. Break off yarn and thread end through these 6 sts. Pull up tightly, secure firmly, and sew finger seam and side seam, leaving last 2¾ in (7cm) open.

Left glove

Work as for right glove to **.

Shape thumb

Row 1 (RS): K22, k into front and back of next st, k2, k into front and back of next st, k28—*56 sts*.

Cont in St st throughout, work 3 rows.

Row 5 (RS): K22, k into front and back of next st, k4, k into front and back of next st, k28—*58 sts*.

Work 3 rows.

Cont to inc in same way, inc 2 sts on next row and every foll 4th row until there are 68 sts.

Work 3 rows.

Next row (RS): K40, turn, cast on 2 sts.

Next row: P20, turn, cast on 2 sts—*22 sts*.

Complete as for right glove from ***.

Ties (make 2)

Using size 3 (3mm) needles, cast on 18 sts and work 20 in (50cm) in St st.

Bind off.

To finish

Weave in any loose yarn ends. Fold each tie in half lengthwise to find center, then pin center of one tie to center of cast-on edge of each glove. Sew tie to glove along cast-on edge, leaving excess unattached.

Sew side seams and knot tie ends together.

satin crop top

materials

Any fingering-weight silk yarn, such as Jaeger *Silk 4ply*
  2 (3, 3) × 1¾ oz (50g) balls
Pair each of sizes 3 (3.25mm) and 6 (4mm) knitting needles
Approximately 2¼ yds (2m) of satin ribbon, 1 in (2.5cm) wide,
  for shoulder straps

sizes

to fit bust	32–34	36–38	40–42	in
	81–86	91–97	102–107	cm
actual bra-cup	5¾	6¼	7	in
length	14.5	16	17.5	cm
length from tie end	38	44	50	in
to tie end	96.5	112	127	cm

gauge

21 sts and 26 rows = 4 in (10cm) in St st using size 6 (4mm)
  needles or whatever size necessary to obtain gauge and two
  strands of yarn held together

See pages 22–23

satin crop top

pattern note
• Use two strands of the yarn held together throughout.

Right front
Using size 3 (3.25mm) needles and two strands of yarn tog, cast on 38 (44: 50) sts.
Work 4 rows in k1, p1 rib, dec 1 st in center of last row—37 (43: 49) sts.
Change to size 6 (4mm) needles and beg with a k row, work 4 (6: 6) rows in St st.
Next row (RS): K18 (21: 24), M1, k1, M1, k18 (21: 24)—39 (45: 51) sts.
Working in St st throughout, cont to inc 1 st on each side of center st as set on every foll 4th row until there are 43 (49: 55) sts.
Work even for 5 (5: 7) rows, ending with RS facing for next row.

Shape top
Shape top by working short rows as foll:
Next row (RS): K39 (45: 51), bring yarn to front of work between needles, slip next st onto right needle, take yarn to back of work between needles, then slip the slipped st back onto left needle and turn work.
Next row: P35 (41: 47), slip next st onto right needle, take yarn to back of work between needles, then slip the slipped st back onto left needle and turn work.
Cont working 4 sts less on every row as set 8 times more, then turn after last row and k to end.
Next row: P across all sts.
Leave sts on a holder.

Left front
Work exactly as for right front.

Front neck edge
Sew center front seam, using backstitch and stitching tightly to ease in knitting and slightly shorten seam length.
Using size 3 (3.25mm) needles and two strands of yarn tog and with RS facing, work in k1, p1 rib across 86 (98: 110) sts from holders.
Work 3 rows more in k1, p1 rib.
Bind off in rib.

Left back
Using size 6 (4mm) needles and two strands of yarn tog, cast on 26 (29: 31) sts.

Row 1 (RS): K1, p1, k to last st, p1.
Row 2: K1, p to last 2 sts, k1, p1.
Rep rows 1 and 2 once more.
Next row (RS): K1, p1, k to last 3 sts, k2tog, p1.
Cont is St st keeping edge sts as set, work 2 rows.
Next row (WS): K1, p2tog, p to last 2 sts, k1, p1.
Cont as set, dec 1 st at same edge on every 3rd row until 4 sts rem. Dec 1 st at same edge on every foll 4th row twice—*2 sts*.
Next row: K2tog.
Fasten off.

Right back
Using size 6 (4mm) needles and two strands of yarn tog, cast on 26 (29:

31) sts.
Row 1 (RS): P1, k to last 2 sts, p1, k1.
Row 2: P1, k1, p to last st, k1.
Rep rows 1 and 2 once more.
Next row (RS): P1, k2tog, k to last 2 sts, p1, k1.
Cont in St st keeping edge sts as set, work 2 rows.
Next row (WS): P1, k1, p to last 3 sts, p2tog, k1.
Cont as set, dec 1 st at same edge on every 3rd row until 4 sts rem. Dec 1 st at same edge on every foll 4th row twice—*2 sts*.
Next row: K2tog.
Fasten off.

To finish
Weave in any loose yarn ends. Press pieces gently using a warm iron over a damp cloth.
Sew cast-on edges of backs to side seams of fronts, easing in backs to fit.
Cut ribbon into four equal pieces for shoulder straps. Sew one piece to highest point on each bra cup. Tie on bra and mark corresponding positions on bcks for two remaining straps. Sew these straps in place, then tie ribbon straps into bows at shoulder.

checked cloche

materials

Any super-fine-weight metallic yarn, such as Rowan *Lurex Shimmer*
    A: One ¾ oz (25g) ball in pink
Any fine-weight mohair yarn, such as Rowan *Kidsilk Night*
    B: One ¾ oz (25g) ball in black
Pair each of sizes 3 (3mm) and 5 (3.75mm) knitting needles

size

One size

gauge

23 sts and 32 rows = 4 in (10cm) in St st using size 5 (3.75mm)
    needles or whatever size necesssary to obtain gauge and two
    strands of yarn together

See pages 24–25

checked cloche

pattern notes

- Use two strands of B held together throughout.
- Use mattress stitch to sew up hat for a neat finish.

To make hat

Using size 3 (3mm) needles and two strands of yarn tog, cast on 120 sts.

Change to A and work 1 row in k1, p1 rib.

Change to B and work 2 rows in rib as set.

Change to A and work 1 row in rib as set.

Change to size 5 (3.75mm) needles and k 1 row (WS).

Cont in patt as foll:

Row 1 (RS): Using A, k1, *sl 1 purlwise, k2, rep from * to last 2 sts, sl 1 purlwise, k1.

Row 2: Using A, p.

Row 3: Using B, *sl 1 purlwise, k2, rep from * to end.

Row 4: Using B, p.

Rep last 4 rows until hat measures 5 in (12cm) from cast-on edge, ending with WS facing for next row.

Shape crown

Keeping patt correct throughout, shape crown as foll:

Row 1 (WS): [P17, p3tog] 6 times —*108 sts.*

Work 3 rows.

Row 5: [P15, p3tog] 6 times— *96 sts.*

Work 3 rows.

Row 9: [P13, p3tog] 6 times— *84 sts.*

Work 1 row.

Row 11: [P11, p3tog] 6 times— *72 sts.*

Work 1 row.

Row 13: [P9, p3tog] 6 times— *60 sts.*

Work 1 row.

Row 15: [P7, p3tog] 6 times— *48 sts.*

Work 1 row.

Row 17: [P5, p3tog] 6 times— *36 sts.*

Work 1 row.

Row 19: [P3, p3tog] 6 times— *24 sts.*

Work 1 row.

Row 21: [P1, p3tog] 6 times— *12 sts.*

Break off yarn, leaving a long end. Thread end through sts, pull up tightly, and fasten off.

To finish

Weave in any loose yarn ends, leaving long end for seam.

Press gently using a warm iron over a damp cloth.

Sew back seam.

Trim with your favorite brooch.

cable sweater

materials

Any super-bulky-weight wool yarn, such as Rowan *Big Wool*
    8 (8, 9, 10, 11, 11) × 3 ½ oz (100g) balls
Pair each of sizes 11 (8mm) and 17 (12mm) knitting needles
Cable needle
Approximately 5 ½ yds (5m) of sequin trimming (optional)

sizes

to fit bust	32	34	36	38	40	42	in
	81	86	91	97	102	107	cm
actual bust	34	36	40	42	44	48	in
	86.5	91.5	101.5	106.5	112	122	cm
length	17	18	19	20	21	22	in
	43	46	48	51	53.5	56	cm
sleeve seam	17	17 ½	17 ½	18	18	18 ½	in
	43	44.5	44.5	46	46	47	cm

gauge

8 sts and 12 rows = 4 in (10cm) in St st using size 17 (12mm) needles or
    whatever size necessary to obtain gauge

See pages 26–27

cable sweater

stitches

C2F (cable 2 front)
Slip next st onto cn and leave at front of work, k1, k1 from cn.

C6F (cable 6 front)
Slip next 3 sts onto cn and leave at front of work, k3, k3 from cn.

seed stitch
(worked over a multiple of 2 sts plus 1 st)
Row 1: K1, *p1, k1, rep from * to end.
Rep this row.

Back
Using size 11 (8mm) needles, cast on 48 (52: 56: 60: 64: 68) sts.
Work 3 rows k1, p1 rib.
Change to size 17 (12mm) needles and work as foll:
1st, 2nd, 3rd, and 4th sizes only
Row 1 (RS): Seed st 3 (5: 7: 9: –: –), [p2, k2, p2, k6] 3 times, p2, k2, p2, seed st 3 (5: 7: 9: –: –).
Row 2: Seed st 3 (5: 7: 9: –: –), [k2, p2, k2, p6] 3 times, k2, p2, k2, seed st 3 (5: 7: 9: –: –).
Row 3: Seed st 3 (5: 7: 9: –: –), [p2, C2F, p2, k6] 3 times, p2, C2F, p2, seed st 3 (5: 7: 9: –: –).
Row 4: Rep row 2.
Row 5: Seed st 3 (5: 7: 9: –: –), [p2, C2F, p2, C6F] 3 times, p2, C2F, p2, seed st 3 (5: 7: 9: –: –).
5th and 6th sizes only
Row 1 (RS): Seed st – (–: –: –: 7: 9), [p2, k2] twice, [p2, k6, p2, k2] 3 times, p2, k2, p2, seed st – (–: –: –: 7: 9).
Row 2: Seed st – (–: –: –: 7: 9), [k2, p2] twice, [k2, p6, k2, p2] 3 times, k2, p2, k2, seed st – (–: –: –: 7: 9).
Row 3: Seed st – (–: –: –: 7: 9), [p2, C2F] twice, [p2, k6, p2, C2F] 3 times, p2, C2F, p2, seed st – (–: –: –: 7: 9).
Row 4: Rep row 2.
Row 5: Seed st – (–: –: –: 7: 9), [p2, C2F] twice, [p2, C6F, p2, C2F] 3 times, p2, C2F, p2, seed st – (–: –: –: 7: 9).
All sizes
Row 6: Rep row 2.
Row 7: Rep row 3.
Row 8: Rep row 2.
Rep rows 3–8 until back measures 11½ (12: 13: 14: 14½: 15)in (29: 31: 33: 35: 37: 39)cm from cast-on edge, ending with RS facing for next row.
Shape armholes
Keeping patt correct as set throughout, bind off 2 sts at beg of next 2 rows.
Dec 1 st at each end of next 4 (4: 4: 6: 6: 6) rows—*36 (40: 44: 44: 48: 52) sts.*
Work even for 10 (12: 14: 14: 16: 16) rows.
Bind off loosely.

Front
Work exactly as for back.

Sleeves (make 2)
Using size 11 (8mm) needles, cast on 24 (24: 27: 27: 30: 30) sts.

Row 1 (RS): *K2, p1, rep from * to end.

Row 2: *K1, p2, rep from * to end. Rep rows 1 and 2 until sleeve measures 3¼ in (8cm) from cast-on edge, ending with WS facing for next row.

Next row (WS): Rib as set, inc at end of row on 3rd and 4th sizes and each end of row on 5th and 6th sizes—*24 (24: 28: 28: 32: 32) sts.* Change to size 17 (12mm) needles. Work in patt as foll **and at the same time** inc 1 st at each end of 5th and every foll 14th (14th: 14th: 14th: 14th: 16th) row until there are 30 (30: 34: 34: 38: 38) sts, taking inc sts into seed st.

Row 1 (RS): Seed st 3 (3: 5: 5: 7: 7), p2, k2, p2, k6, p2, k2, p2, seed st 3 (3: 5: 5: 7: 7).

Row 2: Seed st 3 (3: 5: 5: 7: 7), k2, p2, k2, p6, k2, p2, k2, seed st 3 (3: 5: 5: 7: 7).

Row 3: Seed st 3 (3: 5: 5: 7: 7), p2, C2F, p2, k6, p2, C2F, p2, seed st 3 (3: 5: 5: 7: 7).

Row 4: Rep row 2.

Row 5: Work as for row 3 but inc at each end and working C6F instead of k6.

Row 6: Work as for row 2 but with 1 extra seed st at each end.

Row 7: Work as for row 3 but with 1 extra seed st at each end.

Row 8: Work as for row 2 but with 1 extra seed st at each end. Rep rows 3–8 until sleeve measures 17 (17½: 17½: 18: 18: 18½)in (43: 44.5: 44.5: 46: 46: 47)cm from cast-on edge, ending with RS facing for next row.

Shape cap

Keeping patt correct as set throughout, bind off 2 sts at beg of next 2 rows—*26 (26: 30: 30: 34: 34) sts.*

Dec 1 st at each end of next and every foll alt row until 8 (10: 12: 10: 12: 11) sts rem.
Work 1 row.
Bind off.

To finish

Weave in any loose yarn ends.
Lay work out flat and gently steam.

Sew sleeves into armholes, leaving left back armhole seam open.

Neckband

Using size 11 (8mm) needles and with RS facing, pick up and k 8 (10: 12: 10: 12: 12) sts across top of sleeve, 36 (40: 44: 44: 48: 52) sts across front, 8 (10: 12: 10: 12: 12) sts across top of sleeve, and 36 (40: 44: 44: 48: 52) sts across back—*88 (100: 112: 108: 120: 128) sts.*

Row 1: *P2, k1, rep from * to last 1 (1: 1: 0: 0: 2) sts, p1 (1: 1: 0: 0: 2).

Row 2: K1 (1: 1: 0: 0: 2), *p1, k2, rep from * to end. Rep last 2 rows until rib measures 2½ (2½: 2½: 3¼: 3¼: 3¼)in (6: 6: 6: 8: 8: 8)cm.

Bind off loosely.
Sew left back armhole seam.
Sew side and sleeve seams.
Cut sequin trimming into approximately 25 in (65cm) lengths and sew to cable, weaving under and over following curve of cable and overcast stitching in place by catching in behind sequins.

beaded cuffs and choker

materials

For button cuff

Any super-fine-weight cotton yarn or fine-weight mohair yarn,
such as Yeoman's *Cotton Cannele 4ply* and Rowan *Kidsilk Haze*
One ¾ oz (25g) ball
One spool of fine silver beading wire
Pair of size 3 (3mm) knitting needles
Button for fastening
Assorted buttons, beads, and sequins for decoration
Matching thread for sewing on decoration

For buckle cuff

Any super-fine-weight cotton yarn or fine-weight mohair yarn,
such as Yeoman's *Cotton Cannele 4ply* and Rowan *Kidsilk Haze*
Two ¾ oz (25g) balls
One spool of fine silver beading wire
Pair of size 3 (3mm) knitting needles
Buckle for fastening
Assorted buttons, beads, and sequins for decoration
Matching thread for sewing on decoration

For choker

Any super-fine-weight cotton yarn or fine-weight mohair yarn,
such as Yeoman's *Cotton Cannele 4ply* and Rowan *Kidsilk Haze*
One ¾ oz (25g) ball
One spool of fine silver beading wire
Pair of size 3 (3mm) knitting needles
Approximately 1 yd (1m) of satin ribbon, ⅝ in (1.5cm) wide, for ties
Assorted buttons, beads, and sequins for decoration
Matching thread for sewing on decoration

See pages 28–29 for bracelets and page 31 for choker

beaded cuffs and choker

sizes

Button cuff: approximately 8¾ in (22cm) long by 1¼ in (3cm) wide
Buckle cuff: approximately 9½ in (24cm) long by 1¼ in (3cm) wide
Choker: approximately 11¾ in (30cm) long by 1¼ in (3cm) wide

gauge

29 sts and 39 rows = 4 in (10cm) in St st using size 3 (3mm) needles or
   whatever size necessary to obtain gauge

pattern notes

• Use one strand of yarn with one strand of fine wire held together
   throughout.
• For decoration, collect old buttons and beads of various sizes and
   shapes in your desired color scheme.

To make button cuff

Using size 3 (3mm) needles and one strand of yarn and one strand of wire held tog, cast on 10 sts.
Beg with a k row, work 4 rows in St st.
Make buttonhole as foll:
Next row (RS): K4, bind off next 2 sts, k to end.
Next row: P4, cast on 2 sts, p to end.
Work 6 rows St st, then rep buttonhole rows.
Cont in St st until cuff measures 8¾ in (22cm) (or desired length) from cast-on edge.
Bind off.

To finish

Weave in any loose yarn ends.
Wrap band around wrist, mark where button should fasten, and sew on button.

To embellish

Sew on buttons, beads, and sequins randomly, clustering them together for maximum impact.

To make buckle cuff

Using size 3 (3mm) needles and one strand of yarn and one strand of wire held tog, cast on 4 sts.
Beg with a k row, work 4 rows St st.
Cont in St st throughout, inc 1 st at each end of next row and every foll 6th row twice—*10 sts.*
Work 6¾ in (17cm) on these 10 sts, ending with RS facing for next row.
Shape end of buckle as foll:
Dec 1 st at each end of next and foll 4th row. *6 sts.*
P 1 row.
Bind off.

To finish

Weave in any loose yarn ends.
Thread cast-on edge through buckle bar and sew in place to secure buckle.

To embellish

Sew on buttons, beads, and sequins randomly, clustering them together for maximum impact.

To make choker

Using size 3 (3mm) needles and one strand of yarn and one strand of wire held tog, cast on 8 sts.
Beg with a k row, work in St st until choker measures 11¾ in (30cm) from cast-on edge.
Bind off.

To finish

Weave in any loose yarn ends.
Cut ribbon in half and sew one piece to each end of choker for ties.

To embellish

Sew on buttons, beads, and sequins randomly, clustering them together for maximum impact.

vintage handbag

materials

Any bulky-weight ribbon/tape yarn, such as Louisa Harding
Sari Ribbon or Colinette *Giotto*

  A: One $1\frac{3}{4}$ oz (50g) ball Louisa Harding *Sari Ribbon*

  B: One $3\frac{1}{2}$ oz (100g) hank Colinette *Giotto*

Pair of size 10 (6mm) or size $10\frac{1}{2}$ (7mm) knitting needles

Clasp, approximately 6 in (15cm) wide for ribbed version and $4\frac{1}{4}$ in
(11cm) wide for stockinette stitch version

Piece of fabric for lining, approximately 16 in (40cm) by 12 in
(30cm) for one bag, and matching sewing thread

Approximately 18 in (45cm) of satin ribbon, $1\frac{1}{4}$ in (3.5cm) wide,
for handle for one bag

sizes

Ribbed version: one size, 6 in (15cm) long by 10 in (25cm) wide
across lower edge

Stockinette stitch version: one size, 6 in (15.5cm) long by 7 in
(18cm) wide across lower edge

gauge

Ribbed version: 16 sts and 20 rows = 4 in (10cm) in St st using
10 (6mm) needles or whatever size necessary to obtain gauge
and A

Stockinette stitch version: 12 sts and 21 rows = 4 in (10cm) in
St st using $10\frac{1}{2}$ (7mm) needles or whatever size necessary to
obtain gauge and B

See pages 30–31

vintage handbag

pattern note

• The handbag in the photo is the ribbed version. The stockinette stitch version of the handbag is provided as a quicker alternative.

To make ribbed version of bag

Using size 10 (6mm) needles and A, cast on 26 sts.

Row 1: *K1, p1, rep from * to end.

Row 2: Sl 1 st knitwise, *p1, k into next st but through loop of row below **and at the same time** slip st above off needle, rep from * to last st, p1.

Rep row 2 until bag measures 12 in (30cm) from cast-on edge.

Bind off in rib.

To finish

Cut lining fabric to same size as knitted piece, adding ½ in (1.5cm) all around for seam allowance. Fold knitting in half widthwise with RS together and sew side seams, leaving top end open to attach to clasp.

Sew lining side seams in same way and insert lining into bag. Fold under hem at top of lining and sew in place to top edge of bag. Attach cast-on and cast-off edges of bag to clasp, easing in knitting as required. Sew ribbon handle to clasp or bag.

To make stockinette stitch version of bag

Using size 10½ (7mm) needles and B, cast on 6 sts.

P 1 row.

Next row (inc row) (RS): K1, k into front and back of next st, M1, k to last 3 sts, M1, k into front and back of next st, k2—*10 sts.*

Next row: P.

Rep last 2 rows twice more—*18 sts.*

Cont in St st throughout, work even for 8 rows.

Next row: Rep inc row—*22 sts.*

Work even until bag measures 9½ in (24cm), from cast-on edge, ending with RS facing for next row.

Next row (dec row) (RS): K2, k3tog tbl, k to last 5 sts, k3tog, k2—*18 sts.*

Work even for 9 rows.

Next row: Rep dec row—*14 sts.*

Next row: P.

Rep last 2 rows twice more—*6 sts.*

Bind off.

To finish

Finish as for ribbed version of bag.

cable vest

materials

Any super-fine-weight metallic yarn, such as Rowan *Lurex Shimmer*
   9 (9, 10, 10, 11) × ¾ oz (25g) balls
Pair each of sizes 2 (3mm) and 3 (3.25mm) knitting needles
Size 2 (3mm) circular knitting needle
5 to 7 snaps
5 to 7 mother-of-pearl buttons

sizes

to fit bust						
to fit bust	32	34	36	38	40	42	in
	81	86	91	97	102	107	cm
actual bust	30	32	34	36	38	40	in
	76	81	86	91	97	102	cm
length	17	17	18	18½	19	19½	in
	43	43	45	47	48	50	cm

gauge

32 sts and 32 rows = 4 in (10cm) in single rib using size
   3 (3.25mm) needles or whatever size necessary to obtain gauge
36 sts and 32 rows = 4 in (10cm) in cable patt using size
   3 (3.25mm) needles or whatever size necessary to obtain gauge

See pages 32–33

cable vest

stitches

C2F (cable 2 front)
Slip next st onto cn and leave at front of work, k1, k1 from cn.

C6F (cable 6 front)
Slip next 3 sts onto cn and leave at front of work, k3, k3 from cn.

Back
Using size 3 (3.25mm) needles, cast on 110 (118: 126: 134: 142: 150) sts.
Work in k1, p1 rib throughout as folls:
1st and 2nd sizes only
Inc 1 st at each end of 7th row and every foll 6th row until there are 136 (144) sts.
3rd, 4th, 5th, and 6th sizes only
Inc 1 st at each end of 7th row and every foll 6th and 7th row alternately until there are – (–: 152: 160: 168: 176) sts.
All sizes
Work even until 86 rows have been completed and work measures 9½ (9½: 10: 10: 10: 10½)in (24: 24: 25.5: 25.5: 25.5: 27)cm from cast-on edge.
Shape armholes
Bind off 5 (5: 5: 5: 5: 5) sts at beg of next 2 rows, 4 (4: 4: 5: 5: 5) sts

at beg of foll 2 rows, 3 (3: 4: 4: 4: 4) sts at beg of foll 2 (2: 2: 2: 2: 4) rows, and 2 sts at beg of next 4 (6: 6: 6: 6: 6) rows—*104 (108: 114: 120: 128: 128) sts.*
Dec 1 st at each end of next row and every foll alt row until 98 (102: 106: 110: 114: 116) sts rem.
Work even until armhole measures 7½ (7½: 8: 8½: 9: 9½)in (19: 19: 20: 21.5: 23: 24)cm.
Shape shoulders and neck
Bind off 9 (9: 9: 10: 11: 12) sts at beg of next 2 rows.
Next row: Bind off 9 (9: 10: 10: 11: 11) sts, work until there are 13 (14: 15: 15: 15: 15) sts on right-hand needle, then turn, leaving rem sts on a holder.
Work each side separately.
Bind off 4 sts at beg of next row.
Bind off rem 9 (10: 11: 11: 11: 11) sts.
Rejoin yarn to rem stitches on

holder, bind off center 36 (38: 38: 40: 40: 40) sts and work to end.
Bind off 9 (9: 10: 10: 11: 11) sts at beg of next row and 4 sts at beg of foll row.
Bind off rem 9 (10: 11: 11: 11: 11) sts.

Left front
Using size 3 (3.25mm) needles, cast on 4 sts.
Row 1 (RS): K4, cast on 2 sts—*6 sts.*
Row 2: K1, p5, cast on 3 sts—*9 sts.*
Row 3: P2, k6, p1, cast on 2 sts—*11 sts.*
Row 4: P1, k2, p6, k2, cast on 3 sts—*14 sts.*
Row 5: P1, C2F, p2, C6F, p2, k1, cast on 2 sts—*16 sts.*
Row 6: K1, p2, k2, p6, k2, p2, k1, cast on 3 sts—*19 sts.*
Row 7: K2, p2, C2F, p2, k6, p2, C2F, p1, cast on 2 sts—*21 sts.*
Row 8: P1, k2, p2, k2, p6, [k2, p2]

twice, cast on 3 sts—*24 sts.*

Row 9: K5, p2, C2F, p2, k6, p2, C2F, p2, k1, cast on 2 sts—*26 sts.*

Row 10: P3, k2, p2, k2, p6, k2, p2, k2, p5, cast on 3 sts—*29 sts.*

Row 11: P2, k6, p2, C2F, p2, C6F, p2, C2F, p2, k3, cast on 2 sts—*31 sts.*

Row 12: P5, [k2, p2, k2, p6] twice, k2, cast on 3 sts—*34 sts.*

Row 13: P1, C2F, p2, [k6, p2, C2F, p2] twice, k5, cast on 2 sts—*36 sts.*

Row 14: K1, p6, [k2, p2, k2, p6] twice, k2, p2, k1, cast on 3 sts—*39 sts.*

Row 15: K2, [p2, C2F, p2, k6] 3 times, p1, cast on 2 sts—*41 sts.*

Row 16: P1, k2, [p6, k2, p2, k2] 3 times, p2, cast on 3 sts—*44 sts.*

Row 17: K5, [p2, C2F, p2, C6F] 3 times, p2, k1, cast on 2 sts—*46 sts.*

Row 18: K1, [p2, k2, p6, k2] 3 times, p2, k2, p5, cast on 3 sts—*49 sts.*

Row 19: [P2, k6, p2, C2F] 4 times, p1, cast on 2 sts—*51 sts.*

Row 20: K3, [p2, k2, p6, k2] 4 times, cast on 4 (8: 3: 3: 3: 3) sts—*55 (59: 54: 54: 54: 54) sts.*

Row 21: P2 (6: 1: 1: 1: 1), [C2F, p2, k6, p2] 4 times, C2F, p3, cast on 5 sts (for center front band)—*60 (64: 59: 59: 59: 59) sts.*

Row 22: [P1, k1] twice, p1, k3, [p2, k2, p6, k2] 4 times, p2, k2 (6: 1: 1: 1: 1), cast on 0 (0: 5: 3: 3: 3) sts—*60 (64: 64: 62: 62: 62) sts.*

1st, 2nd, and 3rd sizes only

Row 23 (RS): P2 (6: 6), [C2F, p2, C6F, p2] 4 times, C2F, p3, [k1, p1] twice, k1.

Row 24: [P1, k1] twice, p1, k3, [p2, k2, p6, k2] 4 times, p2, k2 (6: 6), cast on 0 (0: 4) sts—*60 (64: 68) sts.*

Row 25: P2 (6: 10), [C2F, p2, k6, p2] 4 times, C2F, p3, [k1, p1] twice, k1.

Row 26: [P1, k1] twice, p1, k3, [p2, k2, p6, k2] 4 times, p2, k2 (6: 10).

4th, 5th, and 6th sizes only

Row 23 (RS): K2, [p2, C2F, p2, C6F] 4 times, p2, C2F, p3, [k1, p1] twice, k1.

Row 24: [P1, k1] twice, p1, k3, [p2, k2, p6, k2] 4 times, p2, k2, p2, cast on 5 sts.— – (–: –: 67: 67: 67) sts.

Row 25: P1, k6, [p2, C2F, p2, k6] 4 times, p2, C2F, p3, [k1, p1] twice, k1.

Row 26: [P1, k1] twice, p1, k3, [p2, k2, p6, k2] 4 times, p2, k2, p6, k1, cast on 5 sts.— – (–: –: 72: 72: 72) sts.

Row 27: [P2, C2F, p2, k6] 5 times, p2, C2F, p3, [k1, p1] twice, k1.

Row 28: [P1, k1] twice, p1, k3, [p2, k2, p6, k2] 5 times, p2, k2, cast on – (–: –: 0: 4: 8) sts.— – (–: –: 72: 76: 80) sts.

Row 29: P – (–: –: 2: 6: 10), [C2F, p2, C6F, p2] 5 times, C2F, p3, [k1, p1] twice, k1.

Row 30: [P1, k1] twice, p1, k3, [p2, k2, p6, k2] 5 times, p2, k – (–: –: 2: 6: 10).

All sizes

This sets patt, with 5-st k1, p1 rib at center front edge, 5 (5: 5: 6: 6: 6) C2F cables (crossed on every RS row), 4 (4: 4: 5: 5: 5) C6F cable panels (crossed on every 6th row), and 2 (6: 10: 2: 6: 10) sts in rev St st at side-seam edge.

There are *60 (64: 68: 72: 76: 80) sts* and RS is facing for next row.

Side-seam shaping

****Keeping to patt as set throughout, work 2 (2: 6: 6: 6: 6) rows in patt, ending with RS facing for next row. Inc 1 st at beg (side-seam edge) of next row, then at same edge on every foll 6th row 12 times, taking all inc sts into rev St st, ending with WS facing for next row—*73 (77: 81: 85: 89: 93) sts.***

Work even for 5 rows, ending with RS facing for next row.

Neck, armhole, and shoulder shaping

1st and 2nd sizes only

Next row (RS): Bind off 5 sts (at armhole edge), patt to last 8 sts, p2tog, p1, slip rem 5 sts onto a safety pin—*62 (66) sts.*

Work even for 1 row.

To shape armhole, bind off 4 sts at beg of next row, 3 sts at beg of foll alt row, 2 sts at beg of foll 2 alt rows, then dec 1 st at beg of foll 2 alt rows, **and at the same time** beg shaping V-neck by dec 1 st at end (neck edge) of next row and at neck edge on every foll alt row 5 times, ending with WS facing for next row—*43 (47) sts.*

Work even for 1 row.

***Keeping armhole edge straight, dec 1 st at neck edge on next row, then at same edge on every foll alt row twice, then on every foll 3rd row 15 times—*25 (29) sts.*

Work even for 2 rows, ending with RS facing for next row.*******

Next row (RS): Bind off 5 (9) sts, patt to last 2 sts, work last 2 sts tog—*19 sts.*

Work even for 1 row.

Bind off 9 sts at beg of next row—*10 sts.*

85

Dec 1 st at beg of next row.
Bind off rem 9 sts.

3rd, 4th, 5th, and 6th sizes only
Next row (RS): Patt to last 8 sts, p2tog, p1, slip rem 5 sts onto a safety pin— – –: 75: 79: 83: 87) sts.
Work even for 1 row.
Dec 1 st at end (neck edge) of next row, then at same edge on every foll alt row – (–: 0: 0: 1: 2) times— – –: 74: 78: 81: 84) sts.
Work even for 1 row.
To shape armhole, bind off 5 sts at beg of next row, 4 sts at beg of foll alt row, 3 sts at beg of foll alt row, 2 sts at beg of foll 2 alt rows, then dec 1 st at beg of foll 2 alt rows, **and at the same time** cont shaping V-neck by dec 1 st at end (neck edge) of next row and on every foll alt row – (–: 6: 6: 6: 5) times, ending with WS facing for next row— – –: 49: 53: 56: 60) sts.
Work even for – (–: 1: 1: 2: 0) rows.
Keeping armhole edge straight, dec 1 st at neck edge on next row and every foll 3rd row – (–: 17: 19: 19: 19) times— – –: 31: 33: 36: 40) sts.

3rd size only
Work even for 2 rows, ending at armhole edge.
Next row (RS): Bind off 9 sts, patt to last 2 sts, work last 2 sts tog—21 sts.
Work even for 1 row.
Bind off 10 sts. Bind off rem 11 sts.

4th, 5th, and 6th sizes only
Work even for – (–: –: 0: 1: 5) rows, ending at armhole edge.
Bind off – (–: –: 11: 12: 13) sts at beg of next row and foll alt row.
Bind off rem – (–: –: 11: 12: 14) sts.

Right front
Using size 3 (3.25mm) needles, cast on 4 sts.
Row 1 (RS): K4.
Row 2: P4, cast on 2 sts—6 sts.
Row 3: P1, k5, cast on 3 sts—9 sts.
Row 4: K2, p6, k1, cast on 2 sts—11 sts.
Row 5: K1, p2, C6F, p2, cast on 3 sts—14 sts.
Row 6: K1, p2, k2, p6, k2, p1, cast on 2 sts—16 sts.
Row 7: P1, C2F, p2, k6, p2, C2F, p1, cast on 3 sts—19 sts.
Row 8: [P2, k2] twice, p6, k2, p2, k1, cast on 2 sts—21 sts.
Row 9: K1, p2, C2F, p2, k6, p2, C2F, p2, k2, cast on 3 sts—24 sts.
Row 10: P5, k2, p2, k2, p6, k2, p2, k2, p1, cast on 2 sts—26 sts.
Row 11: K3, p2, C2F, p2, C6F, p2, C2F, p2, k5, cast on 3 sts—29 sts.
Row 12: [K2, p6, k2, p2] twice, k2, p3, cast on 2 sts—31 sts.
Row 13: K5, [p2, C2F, p2, k6] twice, p2, cast on 3 sts—34 sts.
Row 14: K1, [p2, k2, p6, k2] twice, p2, k2, p5, cast on 2 sts—36 sts.
Row 15: P1, [k6, p2, C2F, p2] twice, k6, p2, C2F, p1, cast on 3 sts—39 sts.
Row 16: P2, [k2, p2, k2, p6] 3 times, k1, cast on 2 sts—41 sts.
Row 17: K1, [p2, C6F, p2, C2F] 3 times, p2, k2, cast on 3 sts—44 sts.
Row 18: P5, [k2, p2, k2, p6] 3 times, k2, p1, cast on 2 sts—46 sts.
Row 19: P1, [C2F, p2, k6, p2] 3 times, C2F, p2, k5, cast on 3 sts—49 sts.
Row 20: [K2, p6, k2, p2] 4 times, k1, cast on 2 sts—51 sts.
Row 21: P3, [C2F, p2, k6, p2] 4 times, cast on 4 (8: 3: 3: 3: 3) sts—55 (59: 54: 54: 54: 54) sts.
Row 22: K2 (6: 1: 1: 1: 1), [p2, k2, p6, k2] 4 times, p2, k3, cast on 5 sts (for center front band)—60 (64: 59: 59: 59: 59) sts.
Row 23: [K1, p1] twice, k1, p3, [C2F, p2, C6F, p2] 4 times, C2F, p2 (6: 1: 1: 1: 1), cast on 0 (0: 5: 3: 3: 3) sts—60 (64: 64: 62: 62: 62) sts.

1st, 2nd, and 3rd sizes nly
Row 24 (WS): K2 (6: 6), [p2, k2, p6, k2] 4 times, p2, k3, [p1, k1] twice, p1.
Row 25: [K1, p1] twice, k1, p3, [C2F, p2, k6, p2] 4 times, C2F, p2 (6: 6), cast on 0 (0: 4) sts—60 (64: 68) sts.
Row 26: K2 (6: 10), [p2, k2, p6, k2] 4 times, p2, k3, [p1, k1] twice, p1.

4th, 5th, and 6th sizes only
Row 24 (WS): P2, [k2, p2, k2, p6] 4 times, k2, p2, k3, [p1, k1] twice, p1.
Row 25: [K1, p1] twice, k1, p3, [C2F, p2, k6, p2] 4 times, C2F, p2, k2, cast on 5 sts— – (–: –: 67: 67: 67) sts.
Row 26: K1, [p6, k2, p2, k2] 4 times, p6, k2, p2, k3, [p1, k1] twice, p1.
Row 27: [K1, p1] twice, k1, p3, [C2F, p2, k6, p2] 4 times, C2F, p2, k6, p1, cast on 5 sts— – (–: –: 72: 72: 72) sts.
Row 28: [K2, p2, k2, p6] 5 times, k2, p2, k3, [p1, k1] twice, p1.
Row 29: [K1, p1] twice, k1, p3, [C2F, p2, C6F, p2] 5 times, C2F, p2, cast on – (–: –: 0: 4: 8) sts.— – (–: –: 72: 76: 80) sts.
Row 30: K – (–: –: 2: 6: 10), [p2, k2, p6, k2] 5 times, p2, k3, [p1, k1]

twice, p1.

All sizes

This sets patt, with 5-st k1, p1 rib at center front edge, 5 (5: 5: 6: 6) C2F cables (crossed on every RS row), 4 (4: 4: 5: 5: 5) C6F cable panels (crossed on every 6th row), and 2 (6: 10: 2: 6: 10) sts in rev St st at side-seam edge.

There are *60 (64: 68: 72: 76: 80) sts* and RS is facing for next row.

Side-seam shaping

Work as for left front from ** to **.

Work even for 6 rows, ending with WS facing for next row.

Neck, armhole, and shoulder shaping

1st and 2nd sizes only

Next row (WS): Bind off 5 sts (at armhole edge), patt to last 8 sts, k2tog, k1, slip rem 5 sts onto a safety pin—*62 (66) sts.*

To beg V-neck shaping, dec 1 st at beg of next row (neck edge) and at neck edge on every foll alt row 5 times, **and at the same time** shape armhole by casting off 4 sts at beg of foll alt row, 3 sts at beg of foll alt row, 2 sts at beg of foll 2 alt rows, then dec 1 st at armhole edge of foll 2 alt rows, ending with RS facing for next row—*43 (47) sts.*

Work as for left front from *** to ***.

Dec 1 st at beg of next row—*24 (28) sts.*

Bind off 5 (9) sts at beg of next row—*19 sts.*

Work even for 1 row.

Next row (WS): Bind off 9 sts, patt to last 2 sts, work last 2 sts tog.

Bind off rem 9 sts.

3rd, 4th, 5th, and 6th sizes only

Next row (WS): Patt to last 8 sts, k2tog, k1, slip rem 5 sts onto a safety pin— – (–: 75: 89: 83: 87) sts.

Dec 1 st at end (neck edge) of next row, then at same edge on every foll alt row – (–: 1: 1: 2: 3) times— – (–: 73: 77: 80: 83) sts.

Work even for 1 row.

To shape armhole, bind off 5 sts at beg of next row, 4 sts at beg of foll alt row, 3 sts at beg of foll alt row, 2 sts at beg of foll 2 alt rows, then dec 1 st at beg of foll 2 alt rows, **and at the same time** cont shaping V-neck by dec 1 st at beg (neck edge) of every foll alt row – (–: 7: 7: 6: 5) times, and every foll 3rd row – (–: 0: 0: 0: 1) time— – (–: 48: 52: 56: 59) sts.

Work even for – (–: 2: 2: 1: 2) rows.

Keeping armhole edge straight, dec 1 st at neck edge on next row and every foll 3rd row – (–: 17: 18: 19: 18) times— – (–: 30: 33: 36: 40) sts.

Work even for – (–: 0: 1: 2: 6) rows, ending at armhole edge.

Bind off – (–: 9: 11: 12: 13) sts at beg of next row and – (–: 10: 11: 12: 13) sts at beg of foll alt row.

Bind off rem – (–: 11: 11: 12: 14) sts.

To finish

Weave in any loose yarn ends.

Sew both shoulder seams.

Front lapel and collar

Using size 3 (3.25mm) needles and with RS of work facing, rejoin yarn to one set of 5 sts left on safety pin and working in rib as set, inc 1 st at inside edge on next and every foll alt row until there are 30 sts, ending at straight edge.

Bind off first 16 sts, return st on right-hand needle to left-hand needle and cast on 16 sts, rib to end.

Work even until collar fits without stretching to center back neck.

Bind off in rib.

Work other side to match, reversing all shaping.

Picot edgings

Using size 2 (3mm) circular needle and with RS facing, pick up and k 125 (125: 131: 137: 143: 149) sts evenly along edge of armhole.

Work picot edging as foll:

Row 1 (WS): Bind off 3 sts, *slip st on right-hand needle back onto left-hand needle and use to cast on 2 sts using knit cast-on, bind off 5 sts, rep from * to end. Fasten off.

Sew side seams.

Work picot edging around lower edge as foll:

Using size 2 (3mm) circular needle with RS facing, pick up and k 4 sts along left front band, 30 sts along left front slope, 40 (44: 50: 54: 60: 64) sts along other side of left front slope, 106 (112: 118: 124: 130: 136) sts across back, 40 (44: 50: 54: 60: 64) sts along right front slope, 30 sts along other right front slope, and 4 sts along right front band—*254 (268: 286: 300: 318: 332) sts.*

Work picot edging as for armhole edging. Fasten off.

Sew snaps evenly spaced along front edge to start of V-neck shaping. Sew a button on top of each snap.

jacquard scarf

materials

Any bulky-weight wool yarn, such as Debbie Bliss *Maya*
   A: One 3 ½ oz (100g) hank in pink
Any medium-weight wool yarn, such as Rowan *RYC Soft Lux*
   B: One 1 ¾ oz (50g) ball in purple
Any fine-weight mohair yarn, such as Rowan *Kidsilk Haze*
   C: One ¾ oz (25g) ball in lilac
   D: Three ¾ oz (25g) balls in teal
Any bulky-weight wool yarn, such as Debbie Bliss *Maya*
   E: Three 3 ½ oz (100g) hanks in a multi-color
Any bulky-weight ribbon/tape yarn, such as Louisa Harding
   Fauve Tape
   F: Two 1 ¾ oz (50g) balls in green
Pair each of sizes 10 (6.5mm) and 10 ½ (7mm) knitting needles
Approximately 20 in (50cm) of lace (optional)
Beads and sequins (optional)

size

One size, approximately 74 ¾ in (190cm) long by 13 ¾ in
   (35cm) wide

gauge

Each yarn will have a separate gauge; this has been calculated in
   the overall size of the scarf.

See pages 34–35

jacquard scarf

pattern notes

- Use one strand of B held together with one strand of C.
- Use three strands of D held together.
- Use one strand only of A, E, and F.

To make scarf

Using size 10 (6.5mm) needles and one strand of A, cast on 42 sts.

Rib row 1 (RS): [K1, p1] 3 times, *k2, p1, rep from * to end.

Rib row 2: *K1, p2, rep from * to last 6 sts, [k1, p1] 3 times.

Rep last 2 rows until scarf measures 1¼ in (3cm) from the cast-on edge, ending with RS facing for next row.

Change to one strand of B and one strand of C held tog.

Next row (RS): [K1, p1] 3 times, k to end.

Next row: P to last 6 sts, [k1, p1] 3 times.

Rep last 2 rows until BC stripe measures 6 in (15cm), ending with RS facing for next row.

Change to three strands of D held tog.

Keeping to St st with 6-st k1, p1 rib along right edge as set throughout, work until D stripe measures 3 in (7.5cm), ending with RS facing for next row.

Change to one strand of E.

Work until E stripe measures 57 in (145cm), ending with RS facing for next row.

Break off E.

Beg each stripe on a RS row, work D stripe then BC stripe, working same number of rows as before and ending with RS facing for next row.

Change to one strand of A and rep rib rows 1 and 2 until rib measures 1¼ in (3cm).

Bind off in rib.

Edging

Using size 10½ (7mm) needles and one strand of F, cast on 12 sts.

Work in k1, p1 rib until edging fits length of scarf.

Bind off in rib.

To finish

Weave in any loose yarn ends.

Press pieces gently, using a warm iron over a damp cloth and avoiding ribbing.

Sew edging to side of scarf without ribbing.

Cut two random shapes from lace, cutting around lace motifs.

Lay one cut-out lace shape on each end of scarf and sew in place.

If desired, embellish each end of scarf with randomly placed sequins and beads.

chinoiserie cardigan

materials

Any lightweight cotton yarn, such as Rowan *RYC Cashcotton 4ply*
   8 (8, 9, 10, 10, 11) × 1¾ oz (50g) balls
Pair each of sizes 2 (3mm) and 3 (3.25mm) knitting needles
Approximately 1¼ yds (1m) of lining fabric (optional) and matching
   sewing thread
Super-fine-weight metallic yarn or embroidery thread, in bronze,
   for embroidery
Pale pink, pale green, and bronze sequins
Gold bugle beads
7 to 8 snaps
7 to 8 mother-of-pearl buttons

sizes

to fit bust	32	34	36	38	40	42	in
	81	86	91	97	102	107	cm
actual bust	33½	36	38	40	42	44	in
	84	90	95	100	105	110	cm
length	19½	20½	21½	22½	22½	23½	in
	49.5	52	54.5	57	57	60	cm
sleeve seam	12	12½	13	13½	14	14½	in
	30.5	32	33	34	35.5	37	cm

gauge

25 sts and 36 rows = 4 in (10cm) in St st using size 3 (3.25mm) needles or
   whatever size necessary to obtain gauge

See pages 36–37

chinoiserie cardigan

pattern notes

- Work increases and decreases three sts inside the edges and knit through the back of loops to create a fully fashioned detail as follows:

  On a k row: k3, k2tog, k to last 5 sts, k2tog tbl, k3.

  On a p row: p3, p3tog tbl, p to last 5 sts, p2tog, p3.

- Work the center front bands integrally with each front to give a neater finish.

- Increases are made through the sleeve cuffs.

Back

Using size 2 (3mm) needles, cast on 101 (107: 113: 119: 125: 131) sts.

Rib row 1 (RS): *P1, k1, rep from * to last st, p1.

Row 2: *K1, p1, rep from * to last st, k1.

Rep last 2 rows until ribbing measures ¾ in (2cm) from cast-on edge, ending with RS facing for next row.

Change to size 3 (3.25mm) needles and work 12 (14: 14: 16: 16: 18) rows in St st, ending with RS facing for next row.

Cont in St st throughout, dec 1 st at each end of next row and every foll 10th row until 95 (101: 107: 113: 119: 125) sts rem.

Work even for 9 (11: 11: 11: 13: 13) rows, ending with RS facing for next row.

Inc 1 st at each end of next row and every foll 10th (10th: 10th: 12th: 12th: 12th) row until there are 105 (113: 119: 125: 131: 137) sts.

Work even until back measures 12 (12½: 13¼: 13¾: 13½: 14)in (30.5: 32: 33.5: 35: 34: 36)cm from cast-on edge, ending with RS facing for next row.

Shape armhole

Bind off 4 (4: 4: 5: 6: 7) sts at beg of next 2 rows.

Dec 1 st at each end of next 4 (5: 7: 7: 8: 8) rows and then on foll 5 (6: 6: 7: 7: 8) alt rows— *79 (83: 85: 87: 89: 91) sts.*

Work even until armhole measures 7½ (8: 8¼: 8¾: 9: 9½)in (19: 20: 21: 22: 23: 24)cm, ending with RS facing for next row.

Shape shoulders and neck

Bind off 8 sts at beg of next 2 rows— *63 (67: 69: 71: 73: 75) sts.*

Next row: Bind off 8 sts, k until there are 10 (11: 12: 12: 12: 13) sts on right-hand needle, then turn, leaving rem sts on a holder.

Work on these 10 (11: 12: 12: 12: 13) sts.

Bind off 4 sts at beg of next row.

Bind off rem 6 (7: 8: 8: 8: 9) sts.

With RS facing, rejoin yarn to rem sts and bind off 27 (29: 29: 31: 33: 33) center sts, work to end.

Complete to match first side, reversing all shaping.

Left front

Using size 2 (3mm) needles, cast on 54 (57: 60: 63: 66: 69) sts.

Work ¾ in (2cm) in k1, p1 rib as for back.

Change to size 3 (3.25mm) needles and work 12 (14: 14: 16: 16: 18) rows in St st **and at the same time** keep last 5 sts of all RS rows and first 5 sts of all WS rows in k1, p1 rib for center front bands.

Cont in St st throughout, dec 1 st at beg of next row and every foll 10th row until 51 (54: 57: 60: 63: 66) sts rem.

Work even for 9 (11: 11: 11: 13: 13) rows, ending with RS facing for next row.

Inc 1 st at beg of next row and every foll 10th (10th: 10th: 12th: 12th: 12th) row until there are 57 (60: 63: 66: 69: 71) sts.

Work even until front matches back to armhole, ending with RS facing for next row.

Shape armhole

Bind off 4 (4: 4: 5: 6: 7) sts at beg of next row— *53 (56: 59: 61: 63: 64) sts.*

Work 1 row.

Dec 1 st at armhole edge of next 4 (5: 7: 7: 8: 8) rows and then on foll 5 (6: 6: 7: 7: 8) alt rows— *44 (45: 46: 47: 48: 48) sts.*

Work even until 23 (23: 23: 25: 27: 27) rows less have been worked before start of shoulder shaping on back, ending with RS facing for next row.

Shape neck

Bind off 16 sts, work to end of

row—*28 (29: 30: 31: 32: 35) sts.*
Dec 1 st at neck edge on next 2
rows, then on foll 2 (2: 2: 3: 4: 4) alt
rows, then on every foll 4th row until
22 (23: 24: 24: 24: 25) sts rem.
Work even for 9 (9: 9: 9: 9: 13)
rows, ending at armhole edge.
Shape shoulder
Bind off 8 sts at beg of next and
foll alt row.
Work 1 row.
Bind off rem 6 (7: 8: 8: 8: 9) sts.

Right front
Work as for left front, but reverse
all shaping.

Sleeves (make 2)
Using size 2 (3mm) needles, cast on
55 (57: 59: 61: 63: 63) sts.
Work 2¾ in (7cm) in k1, p1 rib as
for back, inc at each end of every
7th row.
Change to size 3 (3.25mm) needles.
Working in St st throughout, cont
to inc 1 st at each end of every
7th row until there are 81 (83: 85:
87: 89: 91) sts.
Work even until sleeve measures
12 (12½: 13: 13½: 13: 14: 14½)in
(30.5: 32: 33: 34: 35.5: 37)cm from
cast-on edge, ending with RS facing

for next row.
Shape cap
Bind off 4 (4: 4: 5: 5: 5) sts at beg
of next 2 rows—*73 (75: 77: 77: 79:
81) sts.*
Dec 1 st at each end of next
4 (5: 7: 7: 7: 7) rows.
Work 1 row.
Dec 1 st at each end of next row
and every foll 2 (2: 3: 3: 4: 4) alt
rows, then on foll alt row until 39
(41: 41: 41: 41: 43) sts rem.
Bind off 4 sts at beg of next 2 rows.
Bind off rem sts.

To embroider
Weave in any loose yarn ends.
Enlarge floral motifs to desired size
on a photocopier (approximately
200%). Use these as templates for
embroidery.
Embroider stems in stem stitch,
using metallic yarn or embroidery
thread. Sew on sequins and beads
where indicated.

To prepare lining
If you wish to line cardigan, lay
lining fabric out flat and trace
outline of each front and back
onto fabric, adding 1¼ in (3cm) all
around for seam allowance.

Cut out each piece, then sew lining
together at shoulders and side
seams and set aside.

Neck edging
Sew shoulder seams.
With RS facing and using size 2
(3mm) needles, pick up and k 37
(37: 37: 38: 39: 39) sts along right
front neck, 35 (37: 37: 39: 41: 41)
sts across back neck, and 37 (37: 37:
38: 39: 39) sts along left front neck
—*109 (111: 111: 115: 119: 119) sts.*
K 1 row.
Bind off knitwise.

To finish
Set in sleeves and sew sleeve and
side seams.
If lining is desired, insert lining and
sew in place, inside selvage edge
along neck, insde ribbing along front
bands and along armhole seam.
Sew buttons to right front band,
positioning them an equal distance
apart. Sew on snaps underneath
button positions.

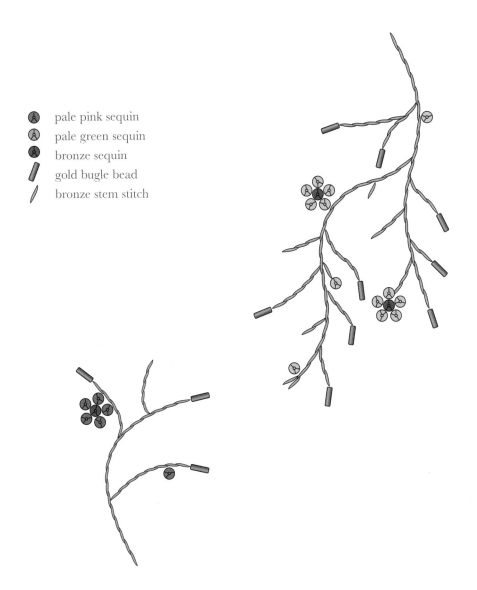

pale pink sequin
pale green sequin
bronze sequin
gold bugle bead
bronze stem stitch

97

embroidered clutch

materials

Any super-fine-weight cotton yarn, such as Yeoman's *Cotton Cannele 4ply*
    A: One 8¾ oz (250g) cone or 372 yds (340m) in ecru
    B: One 8¾ oz (250g) cone or 372 yds (340m) in string
Pair of size 6 (4mm) needles
Approximately ⅓ yd (30cm) of lining fabric and matching sewing
    thread
Approximately 1¼ yds (1.1m) of satin ribbon, 1 in (2.5cm) wide
Gold embroidery ribbon
Lilac, green, and turquoise embroidery thread
Pink beads or sequins

size

One size, approximately 10 in (25cm) long by 6 in (15.5cm) wide

gauge

30 sts and 48 rows = 4 in (10cm) in st patt using size 6 (4mm)
    needles or whatever size necessary to obtain gauge and two
    strands of yarn held together

See pages 38–39

embroidered clutch

pattern note

• Use one strand of A held together with one strand of B throughout.

To make bag
Using size 6 (4mm) needles and one strand of yarn A and one strand of B tog, cast on 75 sts.
Row 1 (RS): K1, *bring yarn to front of work between needles—called *yarn front*—, sl 1 purlwise, take yarn to back of work between two needles—called *yarn back*—, k1, rep from * to end.
Row 2: P2, *yarn back, sl 1 purlwise, yarn front, p1, rep from * to last st, p1.
Rep last 2 rows until bag measures 17¼ in (44cm) from cast-on edge. Bind off.

To embroider
Weave in any loose yarn ends. Press pieces gently using a warm iron over a damp cloth.
Use floral motif on opposite page as a guide for embroidery (it is shown actual size).
Embroider outlines and fill in areas as indicated in diagram, adding beads or sequins as desired.

To line
Cut a piece of lining fabric to same size as bag, adding ½ in (1.5cm) all around for seam allowance. Turn under ½ in (1.5cm) all around and press. Hand sew lining neatly in place to WS of bag.

To finish
Fold in 5½ in (14cm) to WS of bag at one end to make pocket, leaving 6¼ in (16cm) to create flap.
Fold ribbon in half lengthwise and press.
Starting at one corner of pocket, sandwich both layers of bag between ribbon and pin. Sew ribbon in place, making sure that it is even on both sides. Sew ribbon all around edge of bag, mitering corners for a neat finish.

pink glass bead

backstitch in gold ribbon

lilac satin stitch

green satin stitch

turquoise stem stitch

yarns

Although I have recommended a specific yarn for many of the projects in the book, you can substitute others. A description of each of the yarns used is given below.

If you decide to use an alternative yarn, choose a yarn that is of the same weight and type. Purchase a substitute yarn that is as close as possible to the original in thickness, weight, and texture so that it will work with the pattern instructions. Buy only one ball to start with, so you can test the effect. Calculate the number of balls you will need by yardage rather than by weight. The recommended knitting-needle size and knitting gauge on the yarn labels are extra guides to the yarn thickness.

To obtain Colinette, Debbie Bliss, Rowan, or Yeoman yarns, look up the websites given below to find a mail-order supplier or store in your area:

www.uniquekolours.com for Colinette
www.knitrowan.com for Rowan
www.knittingfever.com for Debbie Bliss
www.yarnups.com for Yeoman Yarns

Colinette *Giotto*
A bulky-weight ribbon/tape yarn
Recommended needle size: size 11 (8mm)
Gauge: 11 sts × 16 rows per 4 in (10cm) over St st
Hank size: 158 yds (144m) per 3½ oz (100g) hank
Yarn specification: 50% cotton, 40% rayon, 10% nylon

Debbie Bliss *Maya*
A bulky-weight wool yarn
Recommended needle size: size 9 (5.5mm)
Gauge: 16 sts × 22 rows per 4 in (10cm) over St st
Ball size: 138 yds (126m) per 3½ oz (100g) ball
Yarn specification: 100% wool

Jaeger *Silk 4ply*
A super-fine-weight silk yarn
Recommended needle size: size 3 (3mm)
Gauge: 28 sts × 38 rows per 4 in (10cm) over St st
Ball size: 204 yds (186m) per 1¾ oz (50g) ball
Yarn specification: 100% silk

Louisa Harding *Fauve Tape*
A bulky-weight synthetic ribbon/tape yarn
Recommended needle size: size 10½ (7mm)
Gauge: 20 sts × 28 rows per 4 in (10cm) over St st
Ball size: 127 yds (116m) per 1¾ oz (50g) ball
Yarn specification: 100% nylon

Louisa Harding *Sari Ribbon*
A bulky-weight synthetic ribbon/tape yarn
Recommended needle size: size 11 (8mm)
Gauge: 12 sts × 16 rows per 4 in (10cm) over St st
Ball size: 66 yds (60m) per 1¾ oz (50g) ball
Yarn specification: 90% polyamide, 10% metallic fiber

Rowan *Big Wool*
A super-bulky-weight wool yarn
Recommended needle size: size 19 (15mm)
Gauge: 7.5 sts × 10 rows per 4 in (10cm) over St st
Ball size: 88 yds (80m) per 3½ oz (100g) ball
Yarn specification: 100% merino wool

Rowan *Kidsilk Haze*
A fine-weight mohair-blend yarn
Recommended needle size: sizes 3–8 (3.25–5mm)
Gauge: 18–25 sts × 23–24 rows per 4in/10cm over St st
Ball size: 230 yds (210m) per ¾ oz (25g) ball
Yarn specification: 70% super kid mohair, 30% silk

Rowan *Kidsilk Night*
A fine-weight mohair blend yarn
Recommended needle size: sizes 3–8 (3.25–5mm)
Gauge: 18–25 sts × 23–24 rows per 4 in (10cm) over St st
Ball size: 228 yds (208m) per ¾ oz (25g) ball
Yarn specification: 67% super kid mohair, 18% silk, 10% polyester, 5% nylon

Rowan *Lurex Shimmer*
A super-fine-weight metallic yarn
Recommended needle size: size 3 (3.25mm)
Gauge: 29 sts × 41 rows per 4 in (10cm) over St st
Ball size: 104 yds (95m) per ¾ oz (25g) ball
Yarn specification: 80% viscose, 20% polyester

Rowan RYC *Cashcotton 4ply*

A lightweight cotton-blend yarn

Recommended needle size: size 6 (4mm)

Gauge: 22 sts × 30 rows per 4 in (10cm) over knitted St st

Ball size: 197 yds (180m) per 1¾ oz (50g) ball

Yarn specification: 35% cotton, 25% polyamide, 18% angora, 18% viscose, 9% cashmere

Rowan *RYC Cashsoft DK*

An double-knitting-weight wool-blend yarn

Recommended needle size: size 6 (4mm)

Gauge: 22 sts × 30 rows per 4 in (10cm) over St st

Ball size: 142 yds (130m) per 1¾oz (50g) ball

Yarn specification: 57% merino wool, 33% microfiber, 10% cashmere

Rowan *RYC Soft Lux*

A medium-weight wool-blend yarn

Recommended needle size: size 7 (4.5mm)

Gauge: 19 sts × 25 rows per 4 in (10cm) over knitted St st

Ball size: 137 yds (125m) per 1¾ oz (50g) ball

Yarn specification: 64% merino wool, 10% angora, 24% nylon, 2% metallic fiber

Rowan *Soft Baby*

A medium-weight wool-blend yarn

Recommended needle size: size 7 (4.5mm)

Gauge: 20 sts × 28 rows per 4 in (10cm) over St st

Ball size: 164 yds (150m) per 1¾ oz (50g) ball

Yarn specification: 50% wool, 30% polyamide, 20% cotton

Yeoman *Cotton Cannele 4ply*

A super-fine-weight mercerized cotton yarn

Recommended needle size: size 2 (2.75mm)

Gauge: 33 sts × 44 rows per 4 in (10cm) over St st

Cone size: 930 yds (850m) per 8¼ oz (250g) cone

Yarn specification: 100% cotton

abbreviations

alt	alternate
beg	begin(ning)
cm	centimeter(s)
cn	cable needle
cont	continu(e)(ing)
dec	decreas(e)(ing)
garter st	garter stitch (k every row)
foll	follow(s)(ing)
g	gram(s)
in	inch(es)
inc	increas(e)(ing)
k	knit
m	meter(s)
M1	make one stitch by picking up horizontal loop before next stitch and knitting into the back of it
mm	millimeter(s)
oz	ounce(s)
p	purl
patt	pattern; work in pattern
psso	pass slipped stitch over
rem	remain(ing)
rep	repeat
rev St st	reverse stockinette stitch (p all RS rows, k all WS rows)
RS	right side
skp	slip 1, k1, psso
sk2p	slip 1, k2tog, psso
sl	slip
st(s)	stitch(es)
St st	stockinette stitch (k all RS rows, p all WS rows)
tog	together
WS	wrong side
tbl	through back of loop(s)
yd(s)	yard(s)
yo	yarn over right needle to make a new st
*	repeat instructions after * (or between *) as many times as instructed
**	work up to ** (or between **) as instructed

acknowledgments

My personal thanks and appreciation go to the exceptional people who have collaborated to create this book.

The team at Quadrille Publishing, especially Editorial Director, Jane O'Shea, my mentor, for her constant encouragement and style. Creative Director, Helen Lewis, for her tireless innovation on each new project. Lisa Pendreigh, my wonderful project manager for her rigorous support and inimitable professionalism.

It has been a privilege to have Katya de Grunwald photograph this book; her exceptional and distinctive work, together with stylist Beth Dadswell's unique and inspirational concepts have surpassed my wildest expectations. Thank you also to Anita Keeling our fabulous make-up artist and the beautiful Laure Brosson at Select Model Management.

My heartfelt thanks to Sally Lee, my brilliant project maker, for her constant support, enthusiasm, expertise, and friendship. And of course Eva Yates and Sally Harding for their inestimable and meticulous hard work in pattern checking.

Stephen Sheard of Coats Craft UK for consistently championing me and Kate Buller, brand manager of Rowan Yarns and the team for their generosity and enthusiastic support. Also Tony Brooks of Yeoman Yarns for his invaluable assistance.

Finally, this book is dedicated to 'creatives' everywhere who continually excite with their passion for the hand made and who push the boundaries of craft by their enthusiasm and innovation. You are my constant source of inspiration.